To the People in my life,

Who have given me pain,

Who have given me Joy.

Who,I have Given Pain,

Who,I have Given Joy.

And

Also to those,

Who were JUST THERE.

PIGEONS EVEN SHIT'S ON BUDDHA.

RAAG OF A RECLUSE

SIDHANT BHAGWAT

Made with ♥ on the Notion Press Platform
www.notionpress.com

Contents

Contents

Preface

Art and Philosophy has kept me alive. Life Is about taking a moment and expressing what you feel, This book is the collection of most of my work till now.Whenever I felt someting is accumilating inside I wrote it down(well most of the time,Typed it down).It has helped me to empty myself,just to be filled again. Nothing has lasted,and nothing will last.Maybe i would be the only person to read this book,and may be few more people.And it will get lost in this vast ocean of things.So why to publish it?,why to take efforts to write it at first place?,why to choose to express myself through art?,why to live?,so many why's.why?.

It is just that, I am brought in this existence,and It is upto me to create a Universe for myself.

Thats it.

"Meaning is Just the Sweater which you knit yourself"

1. SIN

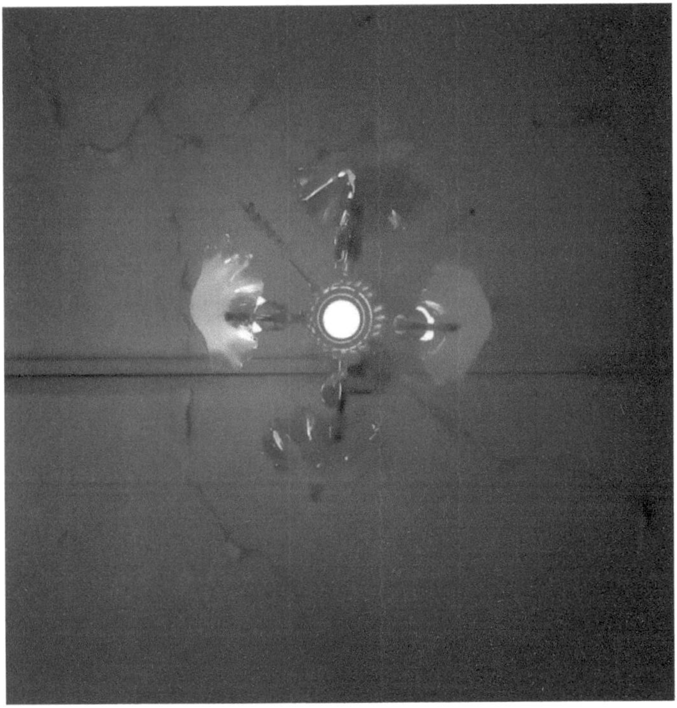

FEBRUARY 26, 2021

SIN

So many sins that I can commit,So many revenges I can take.
So many tears I could cry,
So many promises I can break.
Yet I find myself staring at the ceiling and lying helpless.
While everyone around me shouts,and I act deaf.
When I don't do anything, I feel safe!
Otherwise afraid of the dreams that I see with my eyes open.
Afraid of all the promises that everyone makes.
I like to peel off the healed skin of my wounds.
In this test of life, no one passes, and everybody fails.
It aches suddenly and then it stays for a while.
And the hands shivers
The glass of whiskey shivers
The cell phone shivers.
The pen shivers,
And everything that the hand holds.
Except. the cold heart.
So many tears I could cry, so many promises I could break.
Yet I find myself staring at the ceiling and lying helpless.
While everyone around me shouts,
And I act deaf.
Who Made me Like This?

2. HOUSE

OCTOBER 9, 2019

HOUSE

There lives a fly in their house.
Have you ever noticed the sound of a fly wandering on rotten food?
The way she dances in the air while enjoying her meal, but she rubs her hand every time, i think she is very hygienic.
This kitchen have seen a lot of things, the sizzling sounds that the milk
makes when it overflows and touches the hot flame,
The banging of the utensils when my aunt is angry at her husband.
The lizard staring at the cockroach which is lying dead in the corner of the
gas stove.
But it rained heavily last night and everyone stood still,
my aunt who was in her nighty,
the cockroach who was rock solid like a monument,
the white lizard with a half cut tail,
everyone.
stood still.
No one made any noise,
All that could be heard was the orchestra of the heavy rain drops falling from the sky.
It was Nature again proving its superiority.

Over the turmoil of the,

Man .

Made.

World.

3. MY DARKNESS

AUGUST 4, 2018

MY DARKNESS

Before coming to existence No one asked me,
Do you want to be born?
Before I am going to be dead, No one will ask me,
Do you want to die?
I was brought here without my concern,
And I will be removed without my permission.
Just a small flash of light,and then ages of darkness,then again little light and again lots of
darkness and it goes on and on.
Sometimes I think you just show me light to prove me that it exist but you will not be getting it for
too long.
But it exists. That's it!
And my whole life I will be pleading with you, to show me some light, sometimes even a spark will do.
You want me to be a beggar.
But No!
I know that your light exists,It is beautiful and bright.
It is warm and worth embracing.
Everyone wants it.
Everyone! But not me.
I don't want your light anymore.
I am happy with My darkness.
Because it was there with me even before when I was born, and it will be there with me even after I will die.

Both you and your light are illusions.
I don't want it anymore.
You know! The first time I cried.
I always wondered the reason behind it.
But now I know.
It was because I was separated from my true companion.
Yes, that's the reason why I cried.
But I will be with him again soon,this time forever.
First time when you saw me,there were tears in my eyes,
Last time when you will see me there will be A Smile on my face.
A Smile.
Which will be the answer to all the questions that i ever asked,
And a Question to all the answers that you ever gave.

4. CHAOS

DECEMBER 1, 2017

CHAOS

Chaos everywhere….
Order is just an Illusion.
Crowd of people just running
Some Running to fulfill their daily needs
Some running to fulfill someone else's Greed,

Prisoners of their own emotions
Bounded with the rules and regulations of the society,
Human rules that differ from the rules of
nature.
But sometimes this people think about a lot of things,
Usually when there is an absence of the Sun.
Mainly when they are left alone sometimes at night when there is nobody around them.
They think of some funny and imaginary things some of which is not ethical(You know what I
mean).
For sometime they are in a different world
A world with no human rules, A world where no one is there to judge.
A world full of possibilities.
A world Which is forgotten as soon as the sun rises.
And they are back again to be part of the crowd.
Crowd of people who just run.
Some runs to fulfill their basic needs,
Some run to fulfill someone else's greed.
Chaos everywhere,
And Order?
Order is just an illusion.

5. THERAPY

SEPTEMBER 4, 2022

THERAPY

Dark Thick Blood was dripping from the kitchen knife which his hand was holding sharp blade of knife was reflecting the sun rays and shining like a precious ornament,
no emotions on his face
like someone has poured wet concrete on it days ago
and now it has taken a permanent shape.
Nor any thought in his mind,
and he doesn't even feel motivated to think about anything at that moment .
A fly sits on the nose of the lifeless dead body lying in front of him,
with its mouth open,
The same body which was full of life and energy once but is silent now.
He killed it a few seconds ago.
Just after removing the kitchen knife from its body, He stands and
looks up at the blue sky helplessly and takes a deep breath, and tries to do the breathing exercise
for stress management that his therapist taught him.
He Looks at the body and mummers.
Such
a
stupid
dog,

thought it could make me happy.

6. LIKE ME

DECEMBER 21, 2021

LIKE ME

I have seen a person just like me ruining his life,
writing shit and skipping baths for weeks,
mouth stinking with smell of cigarette
and body shivering due to cold.
But I envy him for his courage to lift the pen and scribble on the paper,
he tries to pour his feelings from a bucket into a teacup full of whiskey,
Blind to see that it is overflowing.
Being wrapped in dirty blanket and trying to breathe.
Eyes about to shut but mind doesn't.
I adore him for his patience.
All I can ask him is a question,why do you do this to yourself ?
And he just smiles and walks away nodding his head and going inside his blanket like a turtle gets inside his Shell trying hard to sleep but the voices in his head don't allow him to be at peace with himself.
And
I
just look at him
and
say
"Such a fool".

7. CHILD

NOVEMBER 22, 2022

CHILD

And in this center of the world,
I feel like being cornered.
By the stupid child inside me.
Wanting to be hugged and driven by id.
And I try to silent him with reason and by shouting on him.
He stays silent until he cannot,
and then he scratches the walls and paints his nails with red color of blood.
I remove him out and take him for a walk.
And I bribe him to stay quiet by giving Not a candy but a glass of Alcohol.
And then he enjoys it and goes to sleep,
until
the
next
episode.

8. LIFE

NOVEMBER 6, 2022

LIFE

Someone asked me where can i see life.
I answered , To see life you have to go to the government hospitals, the police stations, the mental institutions.
This is where you will find the leftovers of the civilization.
The thrash always remains.
The sweet sugarcane juice, leaves dry pulpy Fibrous material, the Beautiful Tea in a cup, leaves behind leftover tea leaves after straining.
The point is, We are evolutionarily designed to forget pain and move forward.
Sometimes it becomes too much for the person and then tragedy occurs.
You will find pain and struggle and tears in those places.
The jail's,
The Crematoriums.
Are the places one should visit after spending joyful moments.
Just to understand the other side of the coin.
And to experience the calmness.
It will help you to close your eyes and see the true nature of the universe.
And there is where,
you will see
life.

9. SMILE

OCTOBER 26, 2022

SMILE

I am finding myself getting aversive to sweetness.
Cat videos make me forget about the stupid problems of my life,
But they don't make the problems go away.
I am learning new things nowadays,
but I don't know what I am learning
and
I can't tell you if you ask me.
It is just the language of feelings which is expressed by the smile,for which people ask me the reason.
And I just nod and say "nothing",
while smiling again.
Life is this and life is that,
you will find many people telling you about it.
Many books,
many philosophers.
But in reality if the voice is not yours,
the answer
will always be a lie.
And At the end of the day all that will matter is if,
You are able to listen to the breath you are taking
or
no.

10. PUZZLE SOLVER

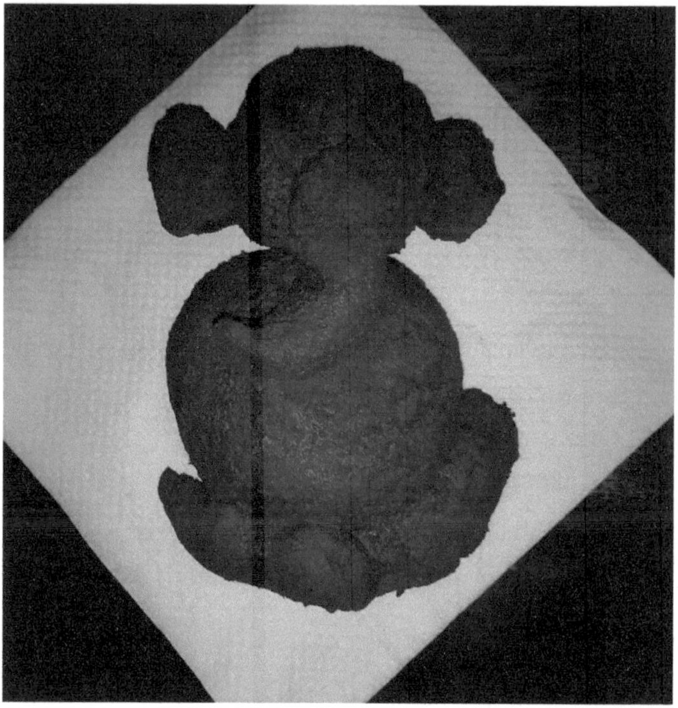

JULY 31, 2022

PUZZLE SOLVER

I Stand in the corner and watch the world with my eyes closed,
I can hear their faces.
But when I open my eyes,
they disappear.
I imagine where they hide.
I find myself alone standing beside my reflection,
We both look at each other and get confused about
who is real
and
who is fake.
We search for the one who will have answer to our question,
and finally we see the
puzzle solver,
But we find him standing in the corner with his eyes closed
and listening to something.

11. ROOM

JUNE 29, 2022

ROOM

I am leaving a part of myself behind,
and taking a part of you with me.
You have heard the voice of my giggles,
and felt the moisture of my tears.
A lot has been learned and a lot has grown inside me.
You have been a great companion and will be alive forever in the neural circuits of my brain.
They might say you are just four walls and a roof,
But for me
you have been much more than someone with flesh and bones.

12. TRAFFIC SIGNAL

JUNE 6, 2022

TRAFFIC SIGNAL

Today,With Her wet hair and a cloth in her hand she gazed and smiled at me, standing on the footpath near the signal. I told myself there is a worth in this non-productive waiting for this red light. That gaze was almost an everyday affair, sometimes the cloth was replaced with dustbin bags and wet hair was replaced with a dirty hat, but the shine on her visible hair remained the same. She used to ask few people if they wanted the bags,but somehow she used to manage to get something out of everyone she decided to approach.She was also used to that lustful touch of people who might be fantasizing about her when they masturbate at night after a hectic day at work. I used to watch her and become numb and imagine how her day would be,and if she is a virgin? Almost not! She was an attractive girl living on a footpath, with a tender age of around 14,15. Maybe she lost her virginity to a drunk rich man at 2PM in the night when she was sold by her parents, or maybe buy a group of local goons that had their eyes on her since she was 10. But today all I could feel was the warmth of that smile, and the smell of the garbage truck in front of me. Both I couldn't escape.

The signal turned green and I was forced to move without a closure.I disliked wasting time on signals, But the next day

I stopped even at the green signal, she came close to me with her hypnotizing gaze, Pink Lipstick on her lips and her black dustbin bags. I asked the price,50 rupees she answered, while we both smiled, I removed the money from my wallet and stopped for a second. Suddenly Blank! Empty! Throat Dry, my eyes were focused on her tender hands, and the next second I found myself holding them. She gave me the bag,denied money, looked down and walked away. That whole day I was sad and thinking about that event, ending up convincing myself that it is just an everyday event for her, nothing big deal. But the next day when I stopped at the signal, I was shocked to notice that everything was the same, the blurred red light, the hot tar road,the filthy voice of the crow sitting on the dead rat, But I noticed 3 things were absent.

Her Gaze.

Her Smile.

And her beautiful Shiny Black Hair.

13. PRIDE

MAY 21, 2022

PRIDE

Everything's ends,
like the last sip of beer in the bottle.
And the last piece of fries in the box.
All that is left is a boutique of memories,
which is garbage for someone else.
But I take the garbage and preserve it like a sacred monument.
And everyone laughs at me.
While some show pity.
But I stand on the mountain of my garbage collection with hands on my hips,
And eyes gazing at the sky.
Displaying great pride on my poker face.

14. MILK

MAY 15, 2022

MILK

I carry some drops of lemon with me,
when a glass of pure milk is served,
unknowingly i put those drops in it.
And ruin it forever.
I hate lemonade.
And the aftermath bitterness that the sugar brings.
I have switched to unnatural plastic to build my nest.
Plastic rhymes with everything these days,
emotions,
feelings,
motives,
Everything.
Biohazard MILK.

15. BALCONY

FEBRUARY 9, 2022

BALCONY

Some people plant roses on their balcony,
Some plant cactus.
While some use their balcony only to dry their dirty Underwear.
And the moon laughs on all of them.
I realized that A road should not be chosen on the basis of, if it's a short cut or a longer route,
not because of how much safe or risky it is to ride,not on the basis of any other stupid analytical thing.
It should be chosen on the basis of how much beautiful the journey will be on it.
I might smell garbage and smile,
some might smell it and puke.
The ability is both a blessing and a curse.
And i enjoy both,
because
one gives meaning to another.

16. CLUB

DECEMBER 4, 2021

CLUB

And this neon lights,
This alcohol influenced cockroaches.
Enjoying their tragedy of life.
Can't feel their heartbeat.
Just a moment of happiness just a moment of Losing their consciousness,
That's all they desire.
Poor fellow.
As soon as the time passes by, they realized that the party of life is over.
And all they are left with, is the routine.
Routine of feeding their soul for a few moments of satisfaction.
It goes on and on.
And
the loop continues
Until
the
Music
Stops.

17. PAPERBOAT

NOVEMBER 10, 2021

PAPERBOAT

And
I have stopped blowing candles for celebration.
I was taught to destroy someone's light,
so that my wish could be granted.
There is no hide and seek anymore.
I have removed all the masks,
And I am fined for that.
Now they force me to wear a mask.
So that I could be the one to put the blame on.
Everyone is trying hard to achieve things that'll not matter when they die.
How much weight can a paper boat carry?

18. PIGGYBANK

MARCH 31, 2022

PIGGYBANK

And you have to run through life,
Crushing the roses
and the ants.
Jumping over walls that are strong and tall,
coz they are built by you yourself.
Finding meaning in life
is like trying to find a penny
in an empty piggy bank.
You lift it.
you shake it.
you turn it upside down.
You are desperate for that penny.
But inside,
Within yourself you know
it is empty,
but the answer is too scary for you.
So you keep shaking the piggy bank all your life,
expecting a sound.
Love the piggy bank as it is,
without expecting a penny out of it.

It will stop raining,
when you will stop finding shelter everytime it rains.

19. SYMPATHY

MARCH 12, 2022

SYMPATHY

In the night,
when the sweet summer breeze kisses my face,
I feel Nauseated and Nervous.
I close my eyes and see a small kid
clenching the fingers of his feets
and listening to his increased heartbeat.
Standing in the door,has got wet in rain,
waiting for someone to pull him close
And dry his hair with empathy.
Finding himself in the middle of a series of fights
that he is dragged in,
creating a Trauma for lifetime.
And when he will grow up
he would be great at
using his shitty life
to gain sympathy.

20. NO

OCTOBER 28, 2021

NO

Make sure you experience enough pain.
Do you think,
you could truly know the true taste of water,
until you are left alone in desert
and starve for 2 days.
And can you be sure,
that you value the brightness of a small candle,
until you are locked in a dark room
and you start scratching the walls.
And can you say,
you truly love someone,
until you have truly seen what life would be
without them.
Things in themselves don't come with any value.
It's the absence of them
that creates one.

21. AGAIN NO

OCTOBER 23, 2021

AGAIN NO

And couple glass of brewed beer in a fancy bar.

Costing more than what 96% of people earn everyday after dedicating their sweat and soul.
And asking a stranger for a favor of cigarette.
And in this moment i ask myself,
What is the difference between me begging for a cigarette,
and a small girl with dirty cloths and mud on her face,
with a skinny baby in her hand, asking for money at the traffic signal.
In some parts of the world at this time someone might not be privileged enough
to taste water.
And here I am, tasting this delicious beer.
the question is that after knowing and feeling all this
Does the taste of the beer and cigarette change for me?
And the answer is I will never know.
Noone will. NEVER EVER.

22. WILD

OCTOBER 21, 2021

WILD

I don't know
but there is something with this world that is wrong.
Some people,some situation,
some rules, some issues.
Can't pinpoint.
But there is something.
Sometimes I just don't know,
Sometimes I don't understand.
All I know is that,
The Smell of water
calms me down.
The sound of birds and wind
makes me smile.
Even if I can't swim
I don't feel afraid.
Its so funny that even when surrounded by a huge chance of danger
I feel safe in the wild.
But this so called safe progressive human society
Scares me.

23. WE

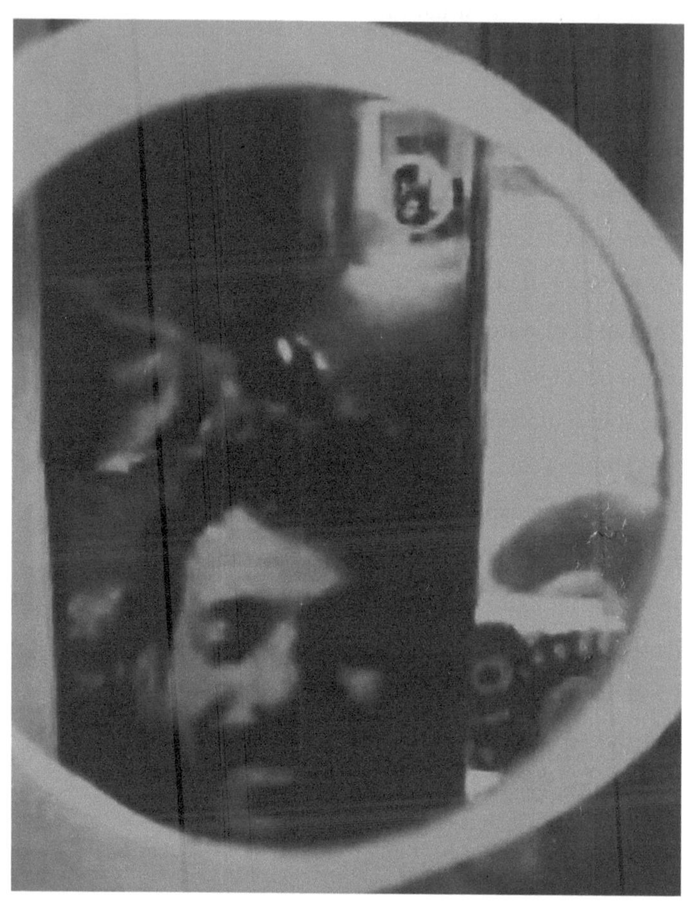

SEPTEMBER 5, 2021

WE

And i will
let you cover my eyes
when I am driving.
We both will rob a bank ,
and fight with someone on the streets
just for fun.
When ur in my arms
there
is
always
a song to write.

24. FREQUENCY

SEPTEMBER 1, 2021

FREQUENCY

Just like the radio,
humans too are tuned to different frequencies,
as according to string theory,
particles and Everything around us is made up of vibration.
Only if we see and feel everything as a bunch of vibration.
We would understand tuning to different frequencies elicits different types of response within us.
Just like the waves our frequency also can get affected by other frequencies
and vice versa.
It's a blissful dance of colorful vibrations.
The intensity depends upon the intensity
of that particular amplitude.
We can try to tune ourselves to that perfect frequency where we can
relate and feel to the fullest, not completely but feel and vibe to as much fullest as possible.
The smells are felt to the core.You can taste water, foods particles to its fullest.
It's a magical feeling.
It's a different kind of high.
Goal should be to maintain that frequency.

25. YZARC

JULY 27, 2021

YZARC

Sweet breeze, sweet smell,
I took candy from the beggars pot.
In motion always, does the friction work here?
Speechless, useless, meaningless,
Will you remember this?
Shouting, Screaming, Whispering,
What difference does it make to a deaf dog?
Full tail, Half cut tail, Or No tail at all,
Why does the lizard stare at me?
Milk, Blood, Wine,
How will their cocktail taste?
Black, Yellow,Pink,
Will They fade with time?
Fear, Dirt, Hope,
What am I breathing?
Not in search of the answers.
Let me Sleep For a While.

26. VOID

JULY 9, 2021

VOID

I have started to feel more comfortable in the void,
used to being there a long time back.
Realized it is just the emptiness that will never leave me alone.
Such a lucky person I am to be blessed with
such a dedicated companion.
Its warm and cozy and it wraps me in its arms of calmness.
I feel no need to go anywhere,
nor to achieve anything.
And I selflessly hug the pillow every single night
even though it doesn't hug me back.
It has gained weight thought,
but I'll not blame it, it's my tears fault.
That's the worst quality of soft things may it be cotton or heart,
it absorbs everything and
keeps it inside,
till it can no more.
Until it becomes useless.

27. OPEN BOOK

MAY 9, 2021

The aim of a wise human,these days.
Must be to become
less human.
Each Face i see,
looks sad and upset.
Battle is most difficult when fought with oneself.
Pleasure Discriminates but Pain is honest.
And Love is a Coin from Devils Wallet.
People wearing colored glasses and Missing the shot.
Everyone Rushing in finding the key to happiness,
But who the fuck told them that the door is locked.
Maybe the one who is trying to sell them locks.
And Brighter the candle burns the sooner it disappears,
Tragedy is an object in the rear view mirror, Closer than it appears.
As a Child used to throw paper planes towards the moon.
Then close my eyes and hope they could make it.
Never smiled for the cameras, I wished I could fake it.
Didn't took sweets from strangers
I was taught not to trust people.
But As I grew old, i knew,
Devil is Good and God is Evil.
Now I talk to dead objects,
even though they can't speak.
I have become an open book

with the language that you can't read.

28. MR.BUBBLEGUM

APRIL 17, 2021

MR.BUBBLEGUM

Mr. Bubblegum, Hello Mr. Bubblegum.
Take me to the lands where milk is black and death is white,
Where stone grows on trees instead of apples.
And butterflies drink blood from wounds instead of nectar from flowers.
Hello,Mr.Bubblegum.
Grab my neck and make this shivering stop,
remove the brain from the skull so that imagination could pause.
Wrap me in thorns gently,
stuff the mouth with broken glass.
Sweet Mr. Bubblegum,
They say you are an angel,
with the ability to bend the fabric of space,and powers to slow down time.
So paint this earth pink, and make everybody blind.
Then finally all the colors of the rainbow could unite.
Hello Mr. Bubblegum,
But first,
Let
me
smile
for
a

while.

29. ROTTEN

APRIL 8, 2021

ROTTEN

It collapses suddenly while you are dreaming and smiling,

All that remains
is silence,
and shallow breath.
Then someone from inside, speaks to you,
it demands to feast on that dirt,
It shouts, Eat it!
Until Nobody is watching.
And you want to lift your hand
to fulfill your hunger,
but you find out that its solid
like a useless monument,
unable to move.
You sit there watching the ants walking in discipline,
the fly rubbing its hands,
The rats racing around in circles,
and the bac-te-ria.
Consuming,
feeding,
Nibbling,
fulfilling the needs of their dying bodies.
Then,You smell the remaining rotten food,
and Discover that
Something
Else
is
also
Rotten.

Ready to be disposed deep underneath.
Ready to be used as a fertilizer.

30. WALK

MARCH 7, 2021

WALK

If you find yourself torn apart between the traumas of the past and the anxieties of the future.
Take a breath.
Tell yourself. No matter what,
You have to walk!
If you feel the people whom you called friends, have left you alone when you were fighting the
storm.Take a breath.
Tell yourself. No matter what,
You have to walk!
If the dagger is inserted in your heart, which you gave to your loved ones.
Hurts on a cold night.
Take a breath.
Tell yourself. No matter what,
You have to walk!
If you feel exhausted,broken and your wounds ache.And find yourself resting alone under the
shadow of a tree.
Take a breath.
Tell yourself. No matter what,
You have to walk!
If you have reached the dead end, and you see a valley of flames in front of you.
Take a breath.

Tell yourself. No matter what,

You.

Have.

To.

Walk.

31. LAUGH

NOVEMBER 17, 2020

LAUGH

Humans cannot digest the fact that this world is meaningless,
And He is not even slightly more valuable
then a filthy cockroach
or
an irritating mosquito.
He will keep distinguishing between good and bad
and valuing his pride and ego
until the time comes
when all the words and man made concepts would have lost
their meaning.
And then
all the creatures that we treated as inferior
will look at us all at the same time,
and Laugh !
And that laughter will be so loud that it will deafen us
forever.

32. EXISTENCE

OCTOBER 25, 2020

EXISTENCE

This whole existence is meaningless!
That means;

All our thoughts and beliefs are unimportant
and useless,
no matter how small
Or big;
how crucial or casual.
So what does that leave us with?
Being so self conscious and monitor our each act
like it'll be rewarded with something,
Or applying a certain kind of mask most of the time.
Life will pass so swiftly
and we will laugh in pity
on our foolishness.
Being one with nothingness and kneeling
in front of the god of uncertainty
is one of the only Wise road
for this journey.

33. CYCLE

MAY 9, 2020

CYCLE

I can still feel the cold air on my face.
Sometimes it used to bring the fragrance of some flowers

and some different things that i can't recognize now.
Me and My Papa used to travel almost everyday a distance of 20 km on his cycle.
He used to drop off me to school in the morning and pick me up in the evening
I used to sit in the front and enjoy the ride everyday.
But as i grew young i felt ashamed of him and his cycle because all my friends' dads had Bikes and cars.
So i started to sit in the back so that no-one would notice me.
And as soon as my school arrived i
used to jump and start walking and tell him to go.
Today that cycle turned 35, He brought it on his 18th birthday.
I wanted to be something better; someone that my Dad would be proud of.
My childish dreams was to buy him a Rolls-Royce Car which scattered as soon as i encountered the real world.
And now i think he would had committed some really worst sins in his past life that he got a son like me.
What can i do? And the answer is Nothing.
I dont know what i will Become.
And i am still ashamed, But Now Not of Him or his Cycle
But of,
Myself.

34. TURMOIL

APRIL 17, 2020

TURMOIL

People are stupid
they Jump,

laugh,
Smile
and are all happy in a moment and then
Fight,
Shout
and Cry in another.
Silently in the Good times they Plan for their own miseries.
Unaware about the tragedies of tomorrow,
They fall in the trap of their own Sensual Pleasures.
Tears of joy & Laughter of sorrows.
I Combine them both, mix it in a glass of whiskey and Sit quietly in the corner of my room.
Sipping and Watching the turmoil of beings.

35. LAUGH

APRIL 13, 2020

LAUGH

If i would have been writing this on a paper,
i would have torn down so many pages,
You might have seen writers doing it in movies.
Yeah just like that,
It feels so Good to do that.
Removing frustration on the same object that helps us express yourself .
But With Smartphone that pleasure is not there.
All you have to do is touch the erase button And it's gone.
That's the problem with Smart and intelligent things;
they experience less emotions.
Time passes and i find myself following the same routine everyday.
Scrolling down on Instagram expecting to see something funny so i could smile , Checking whatsapp for new messages and then realizing that i don't have much friends who would text me.
Chewing and then swallowing the food in the afternoon and then repeating the same in the evening.

And opening the book and reading, but there are different things going around in my mind while i just keep reading the words and just the structure of the words is perceived by the eyes, and the mind doesn't make any sense of it as it is acquired by Random thoughts.

And then i have to read it all over again.

So many things to do but yet so less motivation to do it.

And while thinking about how everyone around me is hindering my growth; seconds pass, minutes pass, followed by hours and another day is gone.

Often at night the introspection is donc.

And Me and My Dreams go to bed together

accompanied by the promises that i made to myself,

While the ghost of uncertainty of life standing near the window Staring at Us with a Big smile,

Laughs....

36. VACUUM

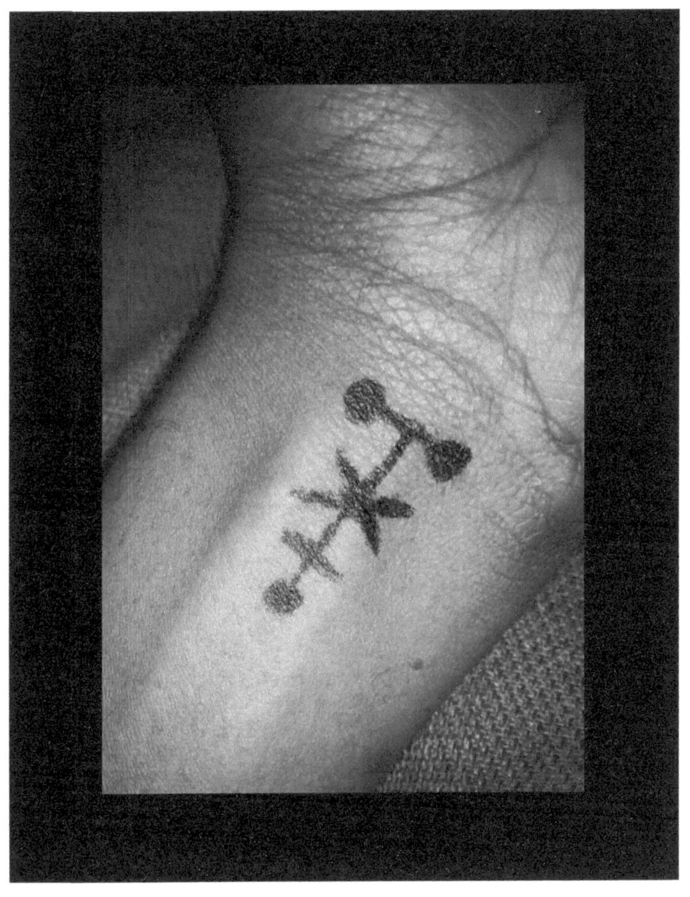

MARCH 25, 2021

VACUUM

All that remains,
is a vacuum.
which tries to pull,
everyone and everything.
that tries to come close to it.
Every ray of light trying a failed attempt to brighten that space
is absorbed and converted into darkness.
It keeps growing,
That Vacuum.
Until, it can expand no more
and then it finally Absorbs itself and
Collapse.
And then Maybe A Star will be born
or
Maybe not.
Nobody knows.

37. “Ek full chicken rice, ek half lollipop”

DECEMBER 31, 2019

"Ek full chicken rice, ek half lollipop".

He gave the order to the Chinese guy who was tossing noodles with an upset face.

It is 31st December and like everybody else he was also unnecessarily excited about the New Year.

though it was only going to be the calendar which was going to be new,

rest everything was going to be in the samc shitty way.

He has been drinking old monk since afternoon and now was having trouble to keep his balance.

Baith jao aap banata hu 5 minute mein said the guy with a used too tone which might have sounded rude to other people but for him it was normal Just because he was under the influence of alcohol.

He sat on the red chair in front of the gas stove so he could have a good view of how the chinese guy was preparing his chicken fried rice.

He gazed at the flames and suddenly became thoughtful.

What is the meaning of all this forced celebration? and all this unnecessary excitement he thought.

Why is it that we have to put on a mask everytime and for whom?

He could feel the warmth of the flame now.

All the memories appeared in the red,blue and yellow flames.

He could see his girlfriend kissing some other guy, His best friends dead body hanging to the ceiling fan, the face of the prostitute with whom he had sex,

The intestines of the dead dog in the middle of the road.

All the dark memories came to life in that flames upon which his food was being cooked.

And all he could do is sit like a Buddha with a helpless smile on his face.

"Ek full chicken rice,ek half lollipop".

Ek sau pachas rupaye hue.

With this voice he suddenly became conscious.

He took the black carry bag and gave the money to him.

And while going,

the Chinese guy shouted.

"Happy new year saheb".

And they both looked at each other

and

smiled.

38. SO FAR

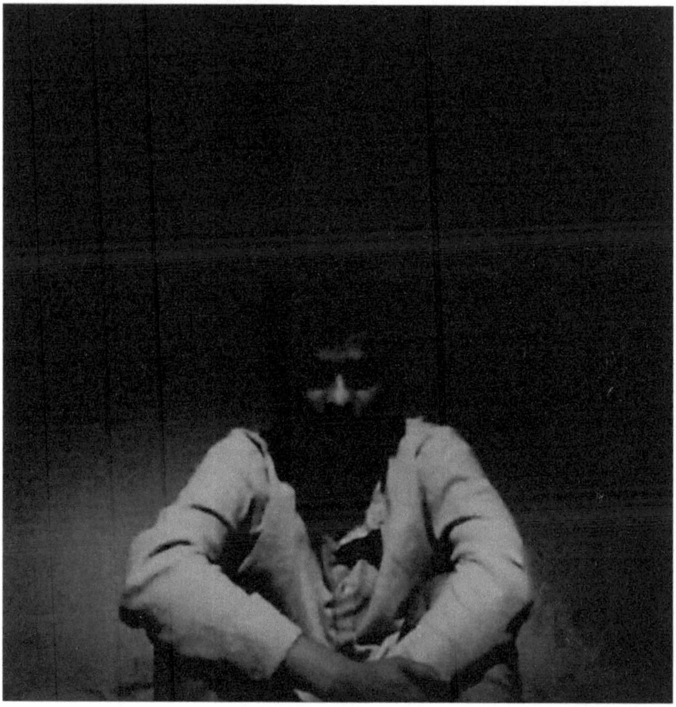

DECEMBER 14, 2019

SO FAR

We have come so far as humans.
From eating the roots of plants,
to ordering food online.
From rubbing stones on each other,
to body temperature sensing Air Conditioners.
From walking barefoot,
to traveling in bullet trains.
So much has changed, Yet we are not happy.
Suicide bombers,
People hanging themself to fans,
Individuals getting admitted in mental institutes.
We are missing something.Something divine, Something pure.
Something that is beyond human mind.
Something which is in sync with the true nature of the universe.
That something can be seen on the face of a crying infant when he is born,
that something can be felt when the dog waves his tail when he expects food.
That something.
Which we experience when we drink water which tastes sweet in the middle of the night, Middle of our dreams.

Something which is beyond human control,
Which is beyond Human understanding.
Something which i don't know yet
Something which you will never know.
Until you take your magical last breath.
Until I take my mysterious last breath.
Only then we will know.
Only then we will understand.
Till then, You know what to do.
Don't you!

39. MOON

NOVEMBER 10, 2019

MOON

The moon looked blurry today.
Is it me or the alcohol?
Or is it that; the moon is fed up of being alone,
Fed up of talking to himself.
And is now killing himself slowly.
Slowly because he doesn't want to hurt the ones who love him.
But is their love not enough?
Yes there are stars but for how long.
When was the last time you gazed at him?
And the truth is that he is ugly as fuck.
And also selfish, He uses the light of the sun.
Has been using it since day one.
And taking all the credit,
Some stupid artist even praised him.
Selfish asshole!
But the sun is also tired now.
And He knows about it.
And he is still silent.
Then why even care for him.
Let him die his lonely death.

But is it really the truth?
Is it me or the alcohol?
Lets See.

40. MASK

JULY 3, 2018

MASK

Everything is moving,
And I am standing there doing a failed attempt
of removing myself from this situation
that I don't want to be.....
Why are you looking at me in such a way?
Haven't you seen a person lost his way?
You should probably look in the mirror.
We Both are same.
I have just
given a different form to my body,
So people could judge me and then they would convince
themself to believe in a false identity of mine.
Just like the false identity and knowledge that
they have about their own and the people around them.
Just look around you
Everyone Is Wearing a Mask,
I am Not The Only One.

41. To Kill A Butterfly

JUNE 10, 2018

I crushed a butterfly under my shoe.
But trust me,
i didn't wanted to.
The butterfly had wings of desire;
Wanted To fly higher

A silly flying insect on the ground,
But eagle in the sky it admired,
It wanted to hug the flower shaped clouds,
wanted to see the world under its wings when he flew.
I crushed the butterfly under my shoe.
You are a fool to leave this garden they said,
You are born to die on the flower they said.
Then they torched him with their words and he became sad in their presence.
They Chained his wings,fragrance had the poisonous essence.
His foolish attempts to escape failed too.
I crushed the butterfly under my shoe.
Now he is lying lifeless on the beautiful soft ground,
Spoiling its beauty with his sad blood making some painful sounds.
He now can see a clear picture of his dream, which earlier was blur.
His only wish now is to close its wings and open it never ever.
At Least his last wish came true,
And i crushed the butterfly under my shoe.
Life! A flower with less honey and more salt in her.
I should have crushed it when it was just a caterpillar
I should have crushed it when it was just a caterpillar.

42. Now a Days

MARCH 18, 2018

NOW-A-DAYS

I don't think about you nowadays
Except when it rains.
Your thought comes in my mind,without my permission
It was raining on the day when i first saw you
You were wearing a red and black salwar kurta that day
Your hair were wet and you looked very beautiful that way,
More beautiful than the rose you were holding in your hand
I forgot to tell you all this at that time.
It's funny how you remember important things when there is no use of it.
So many things are left to say
So many question left to ask
But it doesn't matter now
Because
I don't think about you nowadays
Except when i see strawberry
Your thought comes in my mind
Without My permission
You really loved that red fruit
I never liked it I always thought it was unnecessarily expensive

You also liked almonds,while i preferred groundnuts
And i laughed when you told me that
Oxford Dictionary was your favorite book,
Maybe that was the reason the last time we meet
You had so many words to say
And I was out of words.
But anyways this things doesn't matter now because
I don't think about you nowadays
Except when i see a couple in love
holding each others hand
Your thoughts comes in my mind without my permission.

45. जग किती सरळ

FEBRUARY 1, 2021

जग किती सरळ

शर्पिल्यांनी केले माझ्या हातावरती घाव ,
समदुराच्या लाटांनी चोरले रेतीवरचे नाव
रुसून जेव्हा सावली लांब राहिली पळत
आत्म्याच्या असवांची चव मटिहूनही खारट
गुरु शनी गेले माघे राहिली केवळ अमावस्या
वारा ससाट वेड्यासारखा राहिला पळत दाहीदशि
घरट्याच्या शोधात कोणी दलिा नाही आसरा
कोमेजून रडत बसला पर्याय नाही दुसरा
वासनेच्या पोटी मनुष्य प्राणी झाला लाचार
नैतकितेवर टाकले कापड,
भावनांचा व्यापार
वेडा कलाकार एकटा शूर बाकी सगळे भित्रे
लाटांवरिुद्ध प्रवास सुरु होडीत होते छद्रि
गुलाबानी चेष्ठा केली काटेदेखील हसले
जग किती सरळ उलट्या वटवागळाला दसिले
अंधारात आकाशाला व्यथा माझी सांगतिली
तुटलेला तारा पाहून सुद्धा
मी कोणतीच इच्छा नाही मागतिली
कोणतीच इच्छा नाही मागतिली.

9 798889 752332

Printed by Libri Plureos GmbH in Hamburg,
Germany